IMAGES
of America

HOLYOKE

THE SKINNER FAMILY
AND WISTARIAHURST

IMAGES
of America

HOLYOKE
THE SKINNER FAMILY
AND WISTARIAHURST

Kate Navarra Thibodeau

ARCADIA
PUBLISHING

Published by Arcadia Publishing
Charleston, South Carolina

Library of Congress Catalog Card Number: 2005933679

For all general information contact Arcadia Publishing at:
Telephone 843-853-2070
Fax 843-853-0044
E-mail sales@arcadiapublishing.com
For customer service and orders:
Toll-Free 1-888-313-2665

Visit us on the Internet at www.arcadiapublishing.com

This book is dedicated to my grandparents,
who taught me the value of telling stories, laughing,
and—for heaven's sake—labeling photographs.

CONTENTS

ACKNOWLEDGMENTS

In helping to prepare for this publication, a number of people and institutions deserve acknowledgments. All former interns, researchers, and staff at Wistariahurst Museum have contributed to this book in some form, including those who worked on exhibit research and texts. Elizabeth M. Sharpe's book *In the Shadow of the Dam* provided an in-depth understanding of why William left Williamsburg for Holyoke. Ralmon Black and Eric Weber from the Williamsburg Historical Society guided me through maps and other resources. Other useful resources include Constance McLaughlin Green's history of Holyoke; *The History of the Silk Dyeing Industry in the United States*, by Albert Heusser; *One Morning in May: The Mill River Disaster of 1874*, by Edward C. Jacob; and *Northampton's Century of Silk*, by Marjorie Senechal. Skinner family descendants Allerton Kilborne, Sarah Skinner Kilborne, Mattie Bicknell, and William Bicknell provided photographs, stories, facts, and enthusiastic encouragement. Without them, there would be no book. Also, special thanks go to Sarah Campbell at the History Room at the Holyoke Public Library, who went above and beyond to locate photographs and news articles. Unless otherwise indicated, all the photographs in this book are from the Wistariahurst Museum Archival Collection.

I could not have succeeded without the support of Carol Constant, director of Wistariahurst and an institution herself. She and Melissa Boisselle both encouraged me and indulged in my stories of archival adventure over lunch, asked me probing questions, and pushed me to ask even more questions. To them I say thanks, things at Wistariahurst are "pulpit extra."

To my parents and husband, Bryan, I cannot thank you enough for your constant support and patience. Thank you for being yourselves, loving me, and helping create a history of our own.

INTRODUCTION

"Good history is the history of everybody," stated Ellsworth H. Brown, director of the Wisconsin Historical Society. Historians, educators, curators, and interpreters face the challenge of making history for everybody when researching and writing community histories and presenting them to the public in museums and historic sites. Above all, history is emphasized for the public, often in the form of local and oral history.

There are many ways to learn about the past. One can study the past directly through objects and writings, listen to what people who were there say about the past, and study the present to look for traces of the past.

Wisteria, a flowering vine, covers much of the 26-room mansion, a place where this particular story begins. Wistariahurst features parquet floors, vaulted ceilings, elaborate woodwork, and two marble lions that have guarded the entrance since the late 19th century. But it was not always in Holyoke. The story of the building and the family who lived there begins in Williamsburg in 1868, where the building was constructed for silk manufacturer William Skinner. Local architect William Fenno Pratt designed the house in the traditional Victorian Second Empire style. The house stood in the section of town that was known as Skinnerville, until it was damaged in the Great Mill River Flood of May 16, 1874.

After the flood, William Skinner moved his family and silk-manufacturing business to Holyoke. His home was dismantled and rebuilt at its present site, on Cabot and Beech Streets. In 1908, Belle Skinner and her brother William C. Skinner inherited the house from their mother, Sarah. Belle extensively remodeled the interior, exterior, and gardens. She incorporated several revival styles that dramatically changed the look of the house and grounds. The estate was kept in the family until 1959, when the Skinners gave Wistariahurst to the city of Holyoke for cultural and educational purposes.

Cities that sprang up before and during the Industrial Revolution like Holyoke and Lowell are as different as they are similar. Each city has its own story of colorful characters, financial successes and troubles, entertaining lore, and sometimes tales of woe. The wealth generated from this industrial period in Holyoke allowed the Skinners to rise to the position of local prominence they hold today. Wistariahurst Museum seeks to preserve the home, landscape, and material culture of the Skinner family and Holyoke. The author's hope is that this book continues with that mission and promotes an appreciation of history and culture through these words and images.

Though no amount of research about an historic house is ever truly finished, it is important for the public to know what historians and museum educators know about the past, in this case Holyoke and Wistariahurst. Local history is an interdisciplinary field, and as such, this book utilizes several fascinating resources including documents, photographs, and oral histories. It is the hope of the author that readers of this book become as interested as she has in the process of understanding local history within the context of local, state, national, and international history.

One

THE SKINNER FAMILY

William Skinner (1824–1902) is best known as a prominent silk manufacturer. Skinner used his skill as a silk dyer with tremendous success. His story is one of hard work, dedication, and ingenuity. He is pictured here around 1878, surrounded by his immediate family. Pictured are the following: (first row) Ruth Isabel Skinner, Nancy Skinner, William Skinner, Katharine Skinner, and Joseph Skinner; (second row) Eleanor Skinner, Sarah Allen Skinner, William C. Skinner, and Elizabeth Skinner.

William Skinner was one of the many immigrants who moved to this country and took advantage of the rich resources America offered. He immigrated to America from London, England, at the age of 19. He had learned to dye silk as an apprentice to his father in London. Within about five years, by 1848, Skinner was operating his own silk mill.

Thomas Skinner (1831–1922) (left) followed his two brothers, William and George B. Skinner (1828–1891) (not pictured), to America. He worked as a superintendent in the Skinner Silk Mills in Skinnerville, later moving to Holyoke with his brother William. He was the oldest inhabitant of South Hadley when he died at age 91 in 1922. He is buried in the Village Cemetery of South Hadley Falls.

William Skinner was known as "Old Roman" to his intimates. They described him as having a rugged personality. Skinner's word was never questioned, and he upheld the highest form of integrity in everything he did.

Nancy Edwards Warner (1825–1854) was the first wife of William Skinner. They married in 1848, before William entered a successful business partnership with Joseph Warner in Northampton. Nancy died of marasmus at her sister's house in Ware at the young age of 28. William and Nancy had two children, Eleanor and Nancy.

Sarah Elizabeth Allen Skinner (1834–1908) of Leeds was the second wife of William Skinner. They were married in 1856. Together, they had five children who lived to adulthood. Sarah was devoted to her family, writing each of them almost every day, no matter where they were.

In the 1880s, she introduced two significant features to the exterior of Wistariahurst, the marble lions and the wisteria vine.

Sarah Skinner spent much of her leisure time knitting and writing letters to family. Daughter Ruth Isabel "Belle" Skinner wrote in her journal of January 1878, "Today is mamma's birthday and Joe presented her with some very pretty knitting needles, a present that she needed very much."

Eleanor "Nellie" Skinner (1850–1929), eldest child of William and Nancy, was born in Northampton. She married Frederick H. Warner (1849–1931), a merchant from Boston, on September 8, 1875. Pictured here around 1890, she kept up correspondence with the family, discussing business and family affairs.

Nancy "Nina" Skinner (1852–1922), second child of William and Nancy, married manufacturer Charles E. Clark (?–1917) from Philadelphia in 1880. In 1903, one year after her father died, she wrote to Katharine Skinner Kilborne, "I sent yesterday from the florist addressed to you a wreath of green leaves and carnations. Will you kindly place it on our Father's grave tomorrow the 28th? How quickly the year has flown!"

In letters home to his family, from New York or abroad, William Skinner would often end his correspondence with "now have a good time and don't look backward, your loving husband and Father." (Courtesy of William Bicknell.)

William and Sarah Skinner lived out their lives at Wistariahurst. In 1907, Sarah wrote to her daughter Katharine about Elizabeth taking care of her, "Libbie is walking about on tip toe so afraid she will disturb me after the explicit directions she had not to make a noise to excite me. . . . She is as thoughtful and lovely as possible and I am so glad she is here."

The first son of William and
Sarah Skinner, William Cobbett Skinner
(1857–1947), was born in Williamsburg. In
1876, he joined the family business, working
for the company's sales branch in New York
City. He is shown here in 1896. In 1889, he was
promoted to vice president and sales manager
of the New York City office.

After the death of his father,
William C. Skinner became president.
He was also involved in the New
York, New Haven and Hartford
Railroad, the Pacific Bank of New
York City, the American Surety
Company, and the Silk Association
of America. Pictured here around
1920, he also belonged to the Union
League Club, the Metropolitan
Club, the Automobile Club, and the
Manhattan Club of New York.

Elizabeth Allen "Libbie" Skinner (1859–1927) married Rev. William Hubbard (1851–1913) in 1886 and they lived in Auburn, New York, where she was the head of the missionary societies of the Cayuga Presbytery and organized for the advancement of women in society. After her husband's death, she moved back to Holyoke and was active in her family's church. She died at her home in Holyoke in 1927.

Joseph Allen Skinner (1862–1946), third child of William and Sarah, was born in Williamsburg. He graduated from Yale in 1883 with a bachelor of philosophy degree. Immediately after graduating from Yale, he joined Skinner's Silks and Satins as treasurer. He and his brother, William C., later became partners in the business with their father, and their hard work increased the silk manufacturing business in Holyoke.

In 1887, Joseph Skinner married Martha Hubbard (1862–1934) and soon after moved to South Hadley. They had four children, Ruth Skinner, Elisabeth Hubbard Skinner, William Skinner II, and Martha Skinner.

Joseph Skinner was chairman of the board of the Hadley Falls Trust Company of Holyoke and director of the Holyoke Water Power Company, the New England Telephone and Telegraph Company, and the Old Colony Trust Company of Boston. Locally, he served on the Mount Holyoke College board of trustees for 20 years and received an honorary degree from there in 1925.

17

Ruth Isabel "Belle" Skinner (1866–1928) was educated in the Holyoke public schools before attending Vassar Preparatory in Poughkeepsie, New York, and then Vassar College. She graduated president of the class of 1887, was a member of the Women's University Club of New York and Paris, and was a director of the International Federation of University Women. She is pictured here in 1883.

Belle Skinner was active at Vassar, often performing in plays. This is one of the plays at Vassar College in which she participated in 1887. She is the second "man" in the back row, with her hand raised. The photograph is labeled "Bella always took the leading part."

The Skinner family often camped in Maine for vacation, sometimes traveling to Old Orchard Beach or the Isles of Shoals, off the New Hampshire coast. Shown are Belle Skinner and her companion Pete canoeing across a lake. (Courtesy of William Bicknell.)

In 1908, after her mother's death, Belle Skinner became the woman of Wistariahurst and launched an extensive remodeling and enlargement project that lasted 20 years. She designed the building much as it stands today.

Belle Skinner's first trip to Europe was in 1887. She fell in love with France and was eventually given Le Grande Chancelier de l'Ordre National de la Legion d'Honneur (Legion of Honor) for her work rebuilding the French village Hattonchatel after its destruction in World War I. Villagers lived by the sound of the church bell, which woke them in the morning and rang for village marriages, births, and deaths. They even named the bell, speaking of it as a person. Belle Skinner replaced the bell of the village, and the curé of Hattonchatel named the bell Sarah Isabel after her.

Mary Emma "Baby May" Skinner was born in January 1868 and died only four years later in March 1872. Three other Skinner children died in infancy: Mary Louise, Laura, and Louise.

Katharine "Kittie" Skinner (1873–1968) was the youngest Skinner child. She married Robert S. Kilborne (1874–1950) from Orange, New Jersey, and they spent most of their lives in New York City.

In honor of their father, Katharine and Belle Skinner founded the Skinner Coffee House, a settlement house in downtown Holyoke. On the founding day in November 1902, Katharine stated, "so much is done for the young men in the way of clubs and nothing for the girls that we thought this Coffee House would be a good idea."

Katharine Skinner was Wistariahurst's last full-time resident. In 1958, she wrote, "After a series of conferences it seemed evident our home would be of true value to the City. . . . Therefore, my children and I take great pleasure . . . and are willing to deed 'Wistariahurst' to the City of Holyoke in memory of William and Sarah Skinner. It is our sincere hope, as 'Wistariahurst' has served our family, it may now continue to serve our community."

Skinner siblings Joseph, William C., Belle, Elizabeth, Katharine, Eleanor, and Nancy, although very busy in their own lives, often came together during holidays in the late 1890s. Even when they had families of their own, they still gathered for holidays at Wistariahurst. (Courtesy of William Bicknell.)

The Skinner family posed for this photograph at the Pine Street entrance at Wistariahurst in 1895. Shown from left to right are the following: (first row) Martha Skinner, Elisabeth Skinner, Charles Clark, William Hubbard, Ruth Skinner, and Fred Warner; (second row) Belle Skinner, Elizabeth Skinner, Florence Warner, and Elizabeth Skinner Warner; (third row) Joseph Skinner, William Warner, Eleanor Warner, Nancy Skinner Clark, Raymond Skinner Clark, Katharine Skinner, and William C. Skinner; (fourth row) Fred Warner, Herbert Clark, Sarah Skinner, William Skinner, Edward Hubbard, and Allen Hubbard.

In 1889, it took William C. and his sister Belle from October 30 to November 18 to travel to Japan. On November 4, he wrote, "A chinaman died today—found dead in his bunk, died of Consumption. . . . Belle came down from the deck at 12:30 feeling miserable and is now in bed . . ." Eventually, Belle recovered from her seasickness and both enjoyed a perfectly wonderful trip overseas.

THE CUNARD R.M.S. "CAMPANIA" & "LUCANIA," 12,950 TONS.

On April 17, 1897, Katharine Skinner traveled back from a journey in Europe aboard the *Capania*, a ship whose speed averaged 21.88 knots per voyage. She wrote, "Arrived in New York at 9:30—William was there to meet us and had been since 7:30. Arrived home at 3:50—Happy as a clam. . . . The Holyoke people certainly gave us all a royal welcome and surely there is 'no place like home.'"

Seated on camels in the back from left to right, Katharine, Sarah, and Belle Skinner visited the Sphinx in 1898. Sarah wrote in her journal on February 25, 1898, "Have been out to the pyramids and on our way back stopped at Giza Museum . . . we have had a very pleasant time here and I have rested and the change has done me good . . . I feel perfectly well." The trip took them to Egypt, Jaffa, Beirut, Athens, Naples, and Genoa.

Belle Skinner and William C. Skinner sit on sedan chairs for sightseeing at Wakakusa Hill at Nara, Japan.

Shown above are, from left to right, Katharine, Belle, and Sarah Skinner knitting on the third floor of Wistariahurst in 1898. Sarah wrote in 1904 to Katharine, who was ill, "Am so sorry to hear of your trouble and sincerely hope you are better now as your telegram has informed us just now—we are fine here. All pulpit extra so don't you worry for one moment about us but take the very best care of yourself." The phrases "pulpit extra" or "pulpit double extra" were used by the Skinner family in letters and journals to indicate that everything was fine or very good. Shown below around 1900, Katharine watches while Belle challenges Sarah to a game of checkers in the library, where family members often wrote letters to each other. (Courtesy of William Bicknell.)

Pres. William McKinley attended the graduation ceremony of his niece at Mount Holyoke College in South Hadley and made a trip to Holyoke and the Summit House as a guest of William Whiting. This photograph was taken by a boy on a telegraph pole as the carriage was traveling from the train station to Whiting's house. From left to right are William Skinner, Whiting, and McKinley in a parade on June 17, 1899.

In June 1904, Sarah Skinner wrote to her two daughters Belle and Katharine, "I must write a word to let you know that all is well here—a pretty hot day, but beautiful in our piazza where I have been for the greater part of the morning." In 1904, the piazza, or porch, was at the front of the house on Pine Street.

Robert Stewart Kilborne Jr., often called Stewart, one of Katharine Skinner Kilborne's children, was frequently seen on the grounds of Wistariahurst, leading family members and nursemaids around in his horse-drawn carriage led by a pony named Relief. Belle Skinner purchased Relief for her mother, Sarah, in 1906.

Robert Stewart Kilborne Jr. and his Aunt Belle pet Relief in the gardens at Wistariahurst. Belle Skinner always treated this nephew specially. From Kyoto, Japan, she wrote to him, "My own Sweet-heart, I am so sorry that you have had another illness, and I do hope, Beautiful child, that you are feeling much better today. I am sending you a few little toys . . . Japanese dollies . . . a little doll's house . . ."

The family traveled often, by car or train. When not traveling abroad, Katharine and Belle traveled to Atlantic City, New Jersey. Here, they are having their photograph taken in March 1911.

Belle (left) and William C. took Katharine on her first flight overseas in 1923.

Pictured around 1912 are Katharine Skinner Kilborne and her children William Skinner Kilborne, Elizabeth "Betsy" Allen Kilborne, and Robert Stewart Kilborne Jr. Both William and Robert Stewart later worked at William Skinner and Sons Manufacturing Company. Betsy Kilborne made her debut at a reception held at her home in New York City on November 27, 1926. The Kilbornes later gave her a dinner dance at the Plaza Hotel in December 1926.

Joseph Skinner, Elizabeth Skinner Warner, Katharine Skinner Kilborne, Belle Skinner, and William C. Skinner reveled in laughter and the garden's brilliance in June 1927.

After his wife, Martha, died, Joseph Skinner and his unmarried daughter Elisabeth traveled extensively. Joseph mailed this photograph from India home to his family, stating "Just to show you that your 'little brother' is all right and to tell you that E[lisabeth] and I are having a fine time." A newspaper in 1936 reported that Joseph and his daughter were aboard the *Furness Prince* line bound for South America, stopping at Santos, Rio de Janeiro, Buenos Aires, Santa Lucia, Valparaiso, and Mollendo.

Even into the early 1940s, the family remained close. In his journal of 1941, Joseph Skinner wrote, "Had a fine visit with Will and then to dinner at which Martha, Victor, and Kitten [Katharine] attended. After a fine meal served with cocktails, champagne, and cognac, we, all but Will, went to see the Louisianna [*sic*] Purchase—A fair musical comedy with some catchy music and good dancing."

Joseph Skinner wrote to Kitten in 1941, "I have been up to the house [Wistariahurst] several times and had dinner with Will. He is careful about his eating and drinking, as you wished him to be. The other day when I went up he was sound asleep on the lounge, so you see he is taking Nature's remedy for most everything." Here, they stand in Belle's rose garden at Wistariahurst.

The Skinner family met for a reunion in December 1922. Among those shown are William Kilborne, Louise Hubbard, Sylvia Hubbard, David Hubbard, Allen Hubbard, Ray Clark, Elisabeth Allen Kilborne, Ruth Skinner, Elisabeth Skinner, Margaret Skinner, Helen Clark, Margory Hubbard, Harriet Hubbard (Betsy on lap), Dorothy Hubbard, Elizabeth Hubbard, Belle Skinner, Martha Skinner, Katharine Skinner Kilborne, William Hubbard, Edward Hubbard, Allen Skinner Hubbard, William Skinner II, Robert Stewart Kilborne, William C. Skinner, Joseph Skinner, Charles Clark.

There are four family plots at Forestdale Cemetery in Holyoke. The William Skinner plot holds William, Sarah, William C., and Belle Skinner. The large statue is inscribed with the phrase "death is swallowed up in victory." The Joseph Skinner family plot statue is inscribed "because I live ye shall live also." Buried there are Martha Skinner Logan, Martha Hubbard Skinner, Joseph Skinner, Mary Skinner, William Skinner II, Elisabeth Hubbard Skinner, Walter Henry Hart Jr., Isabel Harris, Ruth Skinner Harris, and David Urquhart Harris. There are also plots for the Kilborne and Hubbard families.

Two

WILLIAMSBURG

On May 16, 1874, a devastating event changed this section of the Connecticut River Valley. When the Mill River Dam gave way that morning, 139 people lost their lives. This is a view of Williamsburg from the west side of the river, looking at the ruins of Spelman's Saw Mill.

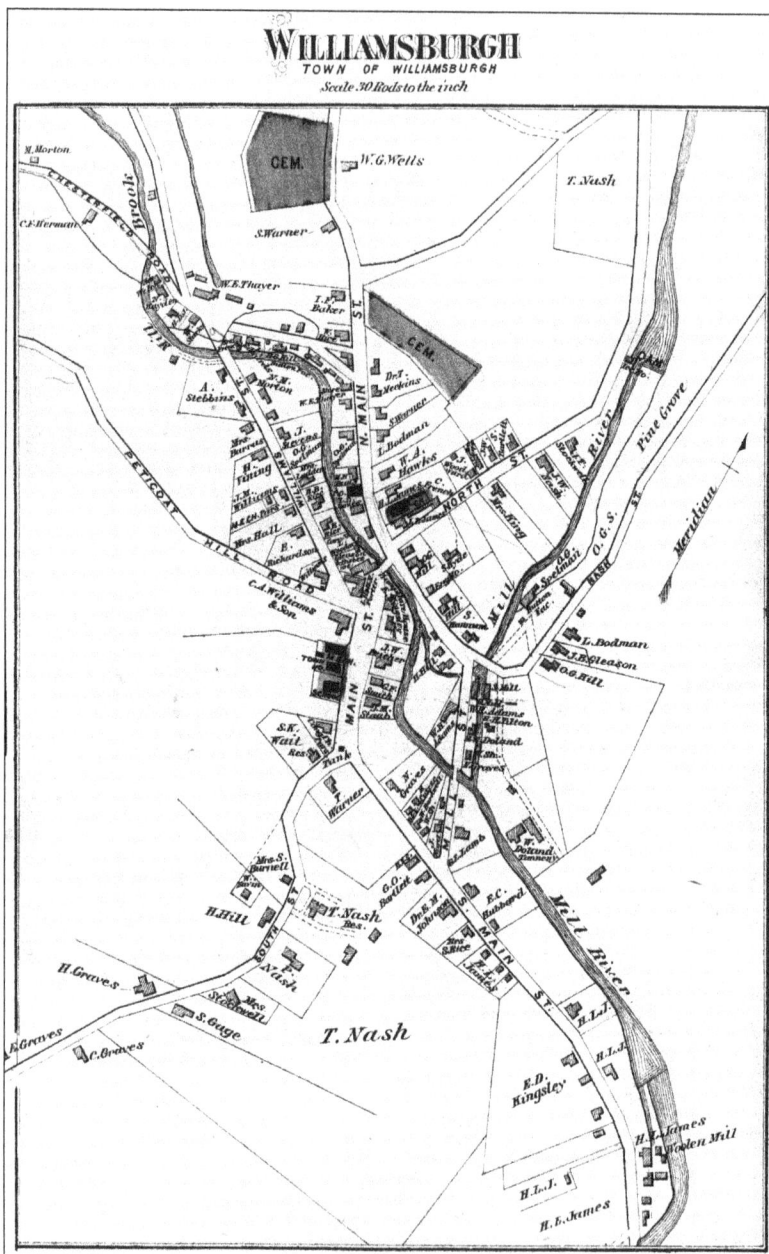

WILLIAMSBURGH
TOWN OF WILLIAMSBURGH
Scale 30 Rods to the inch

Williamsburg was a thriving New England village. Forest-covered hillsides provided timber for construction and fuel. The mills that grew around the Mill River caused villages to grow and families to prosper. When William Skinner arrived in Northampton in 1843, he entered a successfully established silk industry at the Valentine Dye Works. In 1848, however, the business failed and he went into business for himself in a dye house adjoining the Conant Silk Mills. In 1852, Skinner entered partnership with Joseph Warner, establishing a business known as Warner and Skinner in Northampton. When his first wife Nancy died, Skinner's partnership with Warner was dissolved and Skinner moved to Williamsburg to start a business of his own. Skinner employed about 80 people at his Unquomonk Silk Mills, located in the section of town that became known as Skinnerville.

On May 16, 1874, a dam built over the villages of Williamsburg, Leeds, Skinnerville, and Haydenville burst. The water from the flood took about three minutes to get through town. This photograph depicts a pile of debris showing the height of the floodwater as it traveled through Williamsburg.

This is the view at a cove near Williamsburg depot and the wreck of Iron Bridge, where 20 bodies were found in the wreckage.

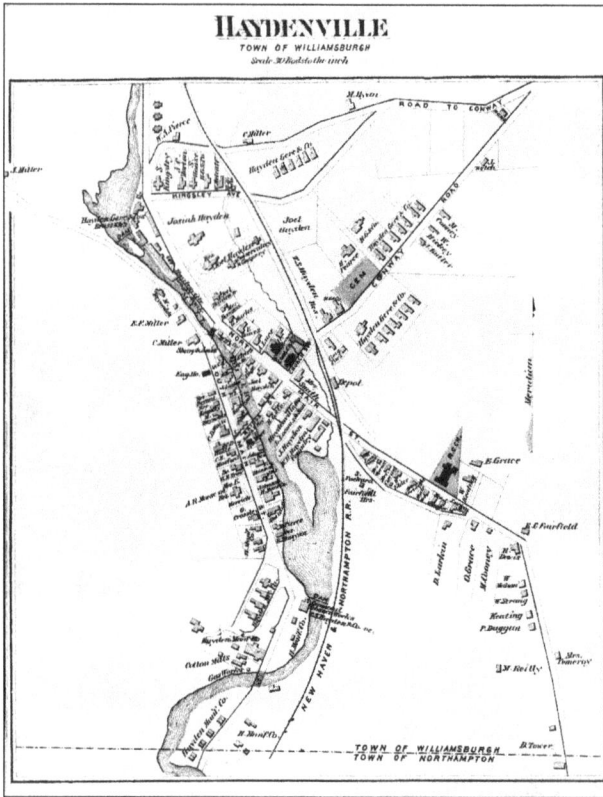

HAYDENVILLE

TOWN OF WILLIAMSBURGH

The town of Haydenville, named for Joel Hayden's mills and factories, was much like Skinnerville, named for William Skinner's silk factories and tenements.

Hayden, Gere, and Company's bank and office were located in Haydenville, shown here before the flood. The company was very successful in manufacturing brass plumbing goods like faucets and valves.

A house slammed up against the wall of Hayden's mill and opened up the side of the brass works. There were two large steam boilers inside the mill. One exploded, and the other was carried over 600 feet downriver.

This is a view looking across the Mill River after the flood in Haydenville.

Businesses in Leeds in 1874 included Northampton Emery Wheel Company; E. S. Ross, a dealer in dry and fancy goods like clothing, groceries, hats, caps, and boots; and George Warner's Ivory Button Company.

The flood hit the town of Leeds a few minutes after 8:00 in the morning.

The houses along a street in Leeds were completely destroyed. A few miles downstream lay dozens of bodies that were carried away by the Mill River.

This is the wreckage of the Nonotuck Silk Mill and the site of two dams and a boardinghouse across the river. The mill was located at the top of Leeds. In the 1920s, the Nonotuck Silk Company merged with a company from New London, Connecticut, to form the Corticelli Silk Company, which subsequently moved its operation to Connecticut.

43

SKINNERVILLE

TOWN OF WILLIAMSBURGH
Scale 30 Rods to the inch

WILLIAMSBURGH DEPOT

M Lawler

Freight Depot

Engine Ho.

Turn Table

W.S.

St Wait Store

Wood Shed R.R.

W.S.

W. Skinner

W.S.

W. S.

Unquomonk Silk Mills

MILL

NEW HAVEN & NORTHAMPTON R.R.

W. Skinner Res.

w.s

J Coogan

SCHOOL

W.Skinner

Lemon

Joseph

Russell

Mrs Stephens

W.S.

T. Bartlett

A Brackenridge

Risley

Skinnerville was located between Williamsburg and Haydenville. Before the flood of 1874, Skinnerville was a town consisting of 35 buildings stretched along a one-half-mile length of the Mill River. It was home to 200 people and William Skinner's Unquomonk Silk Mills, which used the Mill River as power. When the water was low, power was supplied by steam.

In 1854, William Skinner began making silk twists in addition to the original line of sewing skills. To accommodate his growing business, he constructed a three-story mill building in 1857 and named it the Unquomonk Silk Mills, after a local Native American tribe. The company produced organzine, sewing silk, and silk twist for buttonholes. Skinner had 13 boardinghouses in Williamsburg to accommodate his workers.

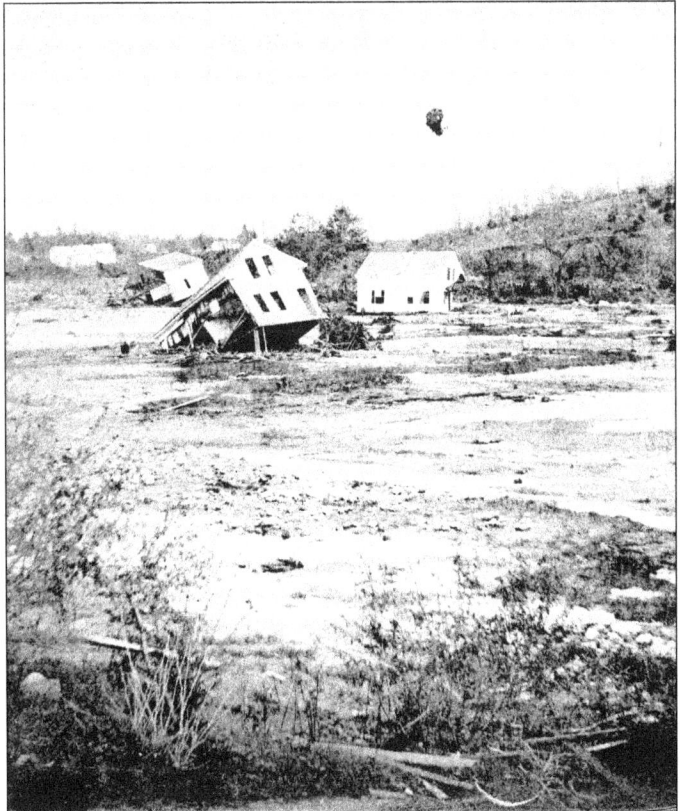

On May 16, 1874, William C. Skinner wrote in his diary, "the men were all standing around in groups . . . [they] said that the Williamsburg Resevoy had given away and had destroyed Williamsburg, Skinnerville & Haydeniville & Leeds & also that 1200 lives were lost. I obtained a team and he driven me home." This is a photograph of the flats in Skinnerville after the Mill River flood.

The dam at Skinnerville, located near the site of the silk mill, did not survive the flood. Two days later, William C. Skinner wrote, "Large gangs of men all day long are digging for bodies." Had Collins Graves not rushed to warn the residents of Skinnerville and Haydenville of the impending flood, William Skinner's mill workers would have perished like so many others.

After the flood, survivors and neighbors from surrounding towns helped scavenge for bodies in the wreckage. William C. Skinner, home from Williston Seminary, searched the remains of the business. On May 22, he wrote, "Jo, Fred, and I went after silk. We found three bales and numerous others of minor importance." The next day he wrote, "Found two more bales and a great many of organized and raw spooled silk."

When William C. Skinner arrived home from Williston Seminary, he learned that his family was safe but had fled to the hills to avoid being washed down by the Mill River. He stated in his diary, "Our house is very nearly the only one standing." Skinner accommodated neighbors and workers who had lost their homes. Mill owners, however, doubted Skinner would rebuild.

In a letter to the editor of the *Springfield Republican*, William Skinner explained, "I have fixed upon Holyoke as my future place of business. . . . Cheap and reliable waterpower is to a manufacturer what good rich land is to a farmer . . . to my dear old friends in Williamsburg: I leave you with a heavy heart, after spending so many happy and prosperous years among you, . . . may the good old town soon recover from the sad calamity now resting upon it."

Skinner dismantled his home and reconstructed it in Holyoke, preparing to rebuild a silk mill along the canals of the Paper City.

Three

INDUSTRY IN HOLYOKE

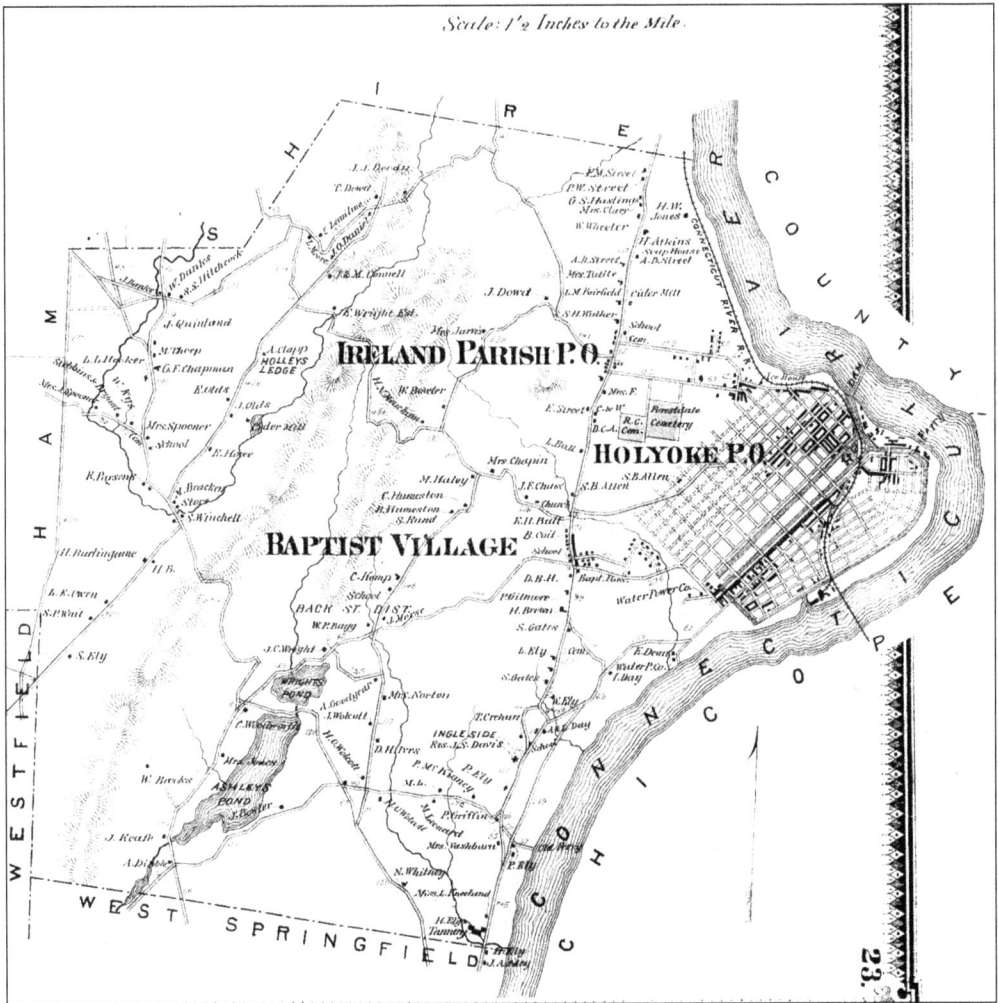

Holyoke was one of the earliest planned cities in America. In 1847, the Boston Associates purchased land in a region called Ireland Parish and took advantage of the 60-foot drop in the river to build a canal system that would provide power for dozens of mills. They named the newly formed city Holyoke for Capt. Elizur Holyoke, who explored the region in 1633.

Construction of the Holyoke Dam began with the Hadley Falls Company in 1847. When the gates were closed to test the strength of the dam, it sprang a leak. That same afternoon, the dam was swept away. The second dam's construction began in 1849, taking seven months to complete. This dam included an apron that supported the base of the dam.

The Holyoke Water Power Company took control of Hadley Falls Company in 1858, when it went bankrupt. Rebuilding a stronger dam with stone was required. This photograph shows the building of the stone foundation for the Holyoke Dam, constructed in the 1890s. A stone foundation was needed to provide more secure force against the powerful flow of the river. The dam was finished in 1900.

The city built around the dam came to be called the Paper City of America, for all of the finish paper manufacturers that were located in Holyoke, beginning in the later 1800s.

This is a view from the air of the Holyoke Dam and South Hadley Bridge. The spillway at the bottom right feeds into the canal system.

The view of the Connecticut River from the air shows green fields, forests, and farms. Holyoke, a city of industry, is pictured in the distance, and the Connecticut River is in the immediate foreground. This photograph was taken from the Summit House of the Mount Holyoke range.

In contrast to the green landscape of the previous photograph, this depicts the industrial development that sprang up along the Connecticut River.

High Street between Dwight and Lyman Streets was the commercial center of Holyoke in the 1890s.

The Merrick brothers from Mansfield, Connecticut, established a thread mill in 1865. By 1871, they had 300 employees. By 1887, they were producing 48 million spools of cotton thread. After Timothy Merrick's death in 1888, the company was sold to a trust called American Thread. The Merrick Thread Mill is shown in a photograph taken from Canal Street.

American Thread Company workers posed in the back of the mill. In 1916, there was a general business expansion during which the capacity was enlarged to 2,000 employees and wages were increased by five percent.

54

The canal system reflected the true arrival of the Industrial Revolution. Canals were needed for the distribution of waterpower to large mills along the river. A survey of canals began in Holyoke in 1847. The canals were built in stages from 1847 to 1893. This is a glass plate negative of the first level canal, from Appleton to Dwight Streets.

The Germania Mills were located on the first level of the canal system. In 1865, two German brothers, Hermann and August Stursberg, started the Germania Mills, a leader in woolen manufacturing. The mill enlarged in 1870, manufacturing heavy fabrics like beavers and doeskins.

The second canal was built 20 feet below the first level. The third level was built 12 feet below the second-level canal. The canal system was dug by hand and is four and a half miles long. This is a postcard of the second level of the canal along the Holyoke Dam.

The paper mills were located on the third-level canal in Holyoke, shown here in 1881. Parson's Paper, established in 1853, was the first paper mill in Holyoke. Whiting Paper Company, established in 1865, was another large paper company. The Valley Paper Company and the Riverside Paper Company were both established in 1866. Albion Paper Company was organized in 1878, and the Nonotuck Paper Company started production in 1880.

The Hadley Thread Mills were built by the Hadley Falls Company, but the building was first used, in 1848 at the time of this photograph, as a machine shop. This view from the back of Lyman Street shows housing for the Hadley Thread Mill workers.

The manufacture of alpaca wool was introduced to England in the 1850s and then spread to Canada, where Herbert Farr learned how to handle the long, tough fibers. The Holyoke Water Power Company financed the building of the Farr Alpaca building in Holyoke and allowed the company 10 years to pay back the debt. By 1874, the machinery was brought in from Canada and the company was up and running. This photograph, taken in 1920, is of the spinning department on Jackson Street. Two of the workers are Stella Baran and Julia Werbiskis.

This is a photograph of the dye house at Farr Alpaca. At the time, women were paid $12 or $14 per week.

National Blank Book, established in 1843, was still one of Holyoke's largest employers in 1969. The company produced school supplies, binders, and other paper gifts. This is a view of young workers swimming at lunchtime in the Connecticut River. The Willamanset Bridge is in the background.

The Crocker Manufacturing Company, shown here in 1881, produced 10 tons of colored paper, books, flats, and specialty papers. Its success is one of the reasons Holyoke is called the Paper City. It was incorporated as the Crocker-McElwark Company in 1901.

The Episcopal Church, established in 1849, is in the center of this photograph, taken in 1863. The city was building not only industry and its interests but also institutions that contributed to Holyoke's culture.

William B. Whiting founded Whiting Coal Company in May 1870, and 75 years later it was still operating under his grandson, Phillip C. Whiting. William Whiting established a business policy of selling the best coal there was and of having efficient service. In 2001, William's great-grandson, Rick Whiting, was president and treasurer of Whiting Oil Corporation, with offices at Lyman Street in Holyoke and King Street in Northampton.

M. J. Doyle Printing Company was a printing and engraving company that began in the late 1890s. It was located on Front Street in Holyoke and advertised having a telephone connection for those needing to contact the company. (Courtesy of William Bicknell.)

In 1842, the Connecticut River Railroad Company was chartered to build a road from Springfield to Northampton. Later, the railroad made a junction at Springfield with other roads from Boston and New Haven, Connecticut. The Boston and Maine Railroad Station was one of many on a rail line from Springfield through Boston and on to Maine. This station was designed and built in 1885 by Henry Hobson Richardson.

High Street was also a commercial center for Holyoke. It was home to shops such as Steigers Department Store. With a number of manufacturing mills moving to Holyoke in the late 1800s, there was a general growth of stores downtown.

Holyoke's town center in the late 1890s and early 1900s was a place for the growth of merchants and dealers in mill supplies. There was also an increase in population and immigration into the city, which created a busier town center.

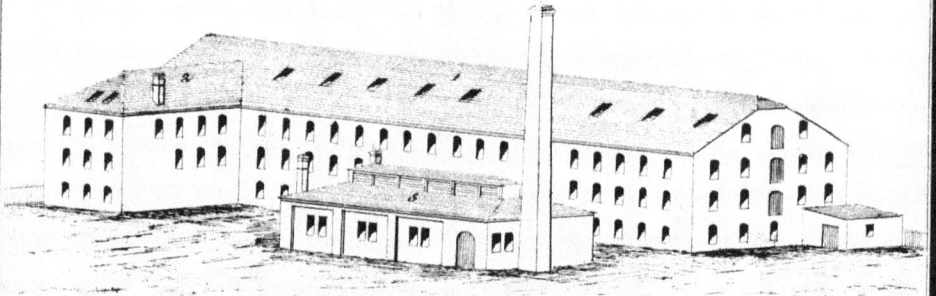

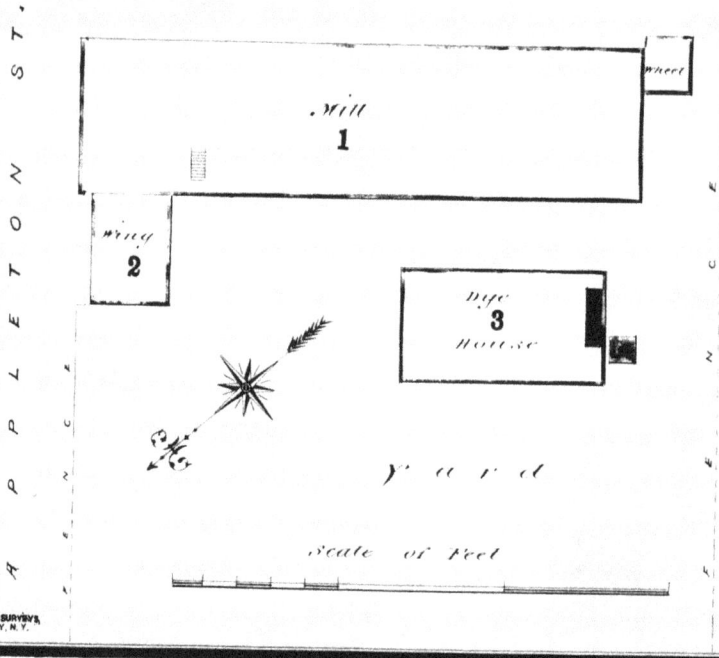

These were the original plans for the new Unquomonk Silk Mills to be built in Holyoke. The Holyoke Water Power Company offered William Skinner a deal he could not refuse. Even though he was 50 years old and was teetering on financial ruin, Skinner was eager to rebuild his business. The city offered a prime canal site, rent free for five years, in which to rebuild his mill. For the price of $1, Skinner could have a one-block portion of land for his home.

Holyoke was building an industrial base in the late 1800s. William Skinner built additional buildings on the canal near the bridge in the 1880s, as seen in this photograph. In the foreground is the beginning of the Westfield Railroad depot.

In October 1874, five months after the Mill River disaster, William Skinner completed his first Holyoke mill and started operations, making the goods with which he was familiar: sewing silk and machine twist. Shortly afterward, he began manufacturing braids and woven goods. As manufacturer of Skinner's satins, his own success was extended to Holyoke and its people.

This is a photograph of the Holyoke Railroad being built behind Skinner's mills. This photograph was taken just after Skinner's Silks and Satins became William Skinner and Sons Silk Manufacturing Company, in 1883.

Four

SKINNER'S SILK
IN HOLYOKE

The Holyoke Water Power Company offered William Skinner a prime canal site, rent free for five years. Within six months of moving to Holyoke, he was producing organzine, a raw silk thread; sewing silk; and twist for buttonholes.

William Skinner's move to Holyoke in 1874 was fortuitous for him and for the city of Holyoke. With an unlimited source of power and inexpensive immigrant labor in Holyoke, the manufacturing business grew to have sales of $6.5 million in the year 1902, with 2,500 employees. Silk and satin were the earliest fabrics produced there and the mainstay business for 87 years.

William Skinner was one of the many immigrants who moved to this country and took advantage of the rich resources America offered. Into the early 1900s, his silk mills provided employment for thousands of Holyokers. His mill was located on the upper canal in Holyoke.

In 1876, William Skinner's eldest son William C. Skinner began working for his father in the New York City office. This office was located at the heart of the city's silk district, at 508 Broadway. Skinner's sons were instrumental in a tremendous business expansion. In this June 1880 photograph, William C. is standing in the doorway.

This photograph was taken outside of 508 Broadway in New York City in April 1885. William C. Skinner, who whould take over the New York City sales office around 1889, is standing directly to the left of the column that holds a sign identifying Skinner as a silk manufacturer.

Gradually, William Skinner added to his original mill building. His son Joseph Allen Skinner joined the business in 1883, and in 1889, William incorporated the business as William Skinner and Sons Manufacturing Company. This photograph, taken in 1890, includes ? Curran, ? Smith, ? Gifford, ? Mooney, ? Gortz, Tom Skinner, Cloveuer Bridges, George Monroe, Alex Williamson, Joseph Skinner, and Charles Roberts.

With just silk braids and threads for sewing silk, William Skinner and Sons Manufacturing Company had stores in New York City and Chicago.

William Skinner and his sons made it a point to travel to other producers and manufacturers of silk to examine the quality and quantity being produced around the world. This was a Japanese business dinner at the Maple Club; William C. is shaking hands with Mr. Shiti.

Finding that sources of raw silk made in America were expensive and of varying quality, William Skinner began to trade directly with Japanese silk traders, including the Sano Raw Silk Manufactory in Japan, shown here.

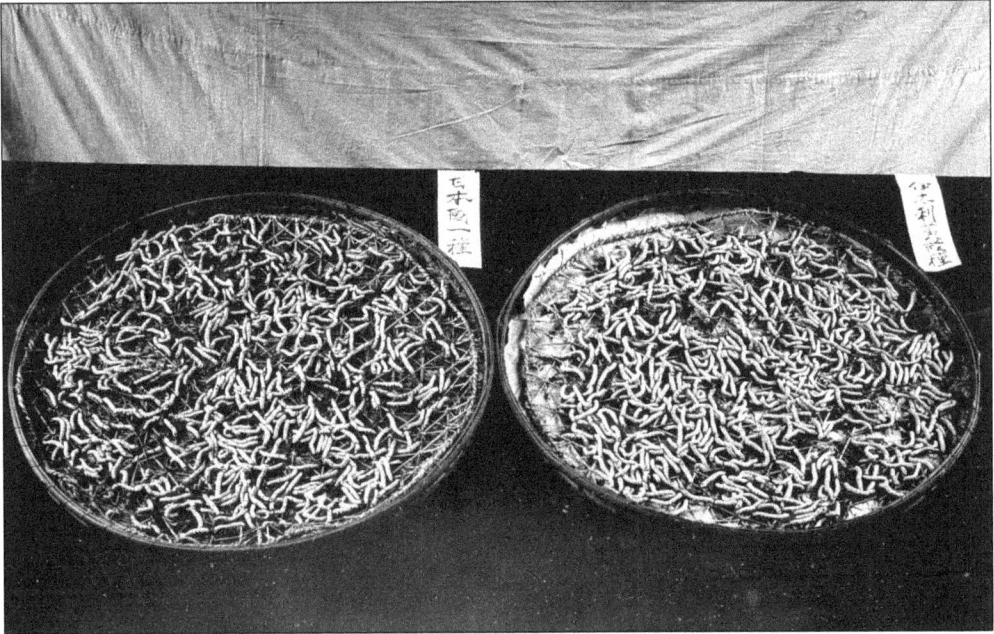

Silk is a natural protein fiber that comes from a *Bombyx mori* moth. Once the cocoon is spun, it is heated to remove moisture. A female moth lays as many as 500 eggs, which hatch into caterpillars in 20 days. In this photograph, Italian yellow cocoons and Japanese Kuniichi cocoons await sorting in the model silkworm rearing house at Sano's.

Caterpillars eat mulberry leaves before they go to cocoon. Here they are kept clean with plenty of circulating air to prevent disease.

Each caterpillar sends a strand of liquid from its mouth that solidifies when it contacts the air. The caterpillar spins a cocoon by moving its head in a figure eight. In two days, the caterpillar becomes completely sealed within a white, egg-shaped cocoon.

Once the cocoon is spun, it is heated to remove the moisture inside the cocoon. Then the finest cocoons are selected for quality silks. The filaments are unwound from the cocoon by being placed in hot water. The threads are reeled together to create thicker and heavier strands.

74

Once dried, each raw silk length is twisted into skeins and packaged in bundles called books, which are then shipped to the manufacturing factory. After the baled raw silk arrived at the Skinner silk mills, it was inspected, sorted, and soaked to soften the strands of fiber.

After twisting, the raw silk is wound back into skeins for dyeing. Emile Housechild was a chemist for the Skinner mills. A chemist mixed dyes to the desired color. The most-used chemicals in silk dyeing are mineral acids. Hydrochloric acid was used for washing in the boiling-off process. For dyeing blacks, hydrochloric acid was a valuable agent. Nitric acid was used chiefly in the bleaching processes.

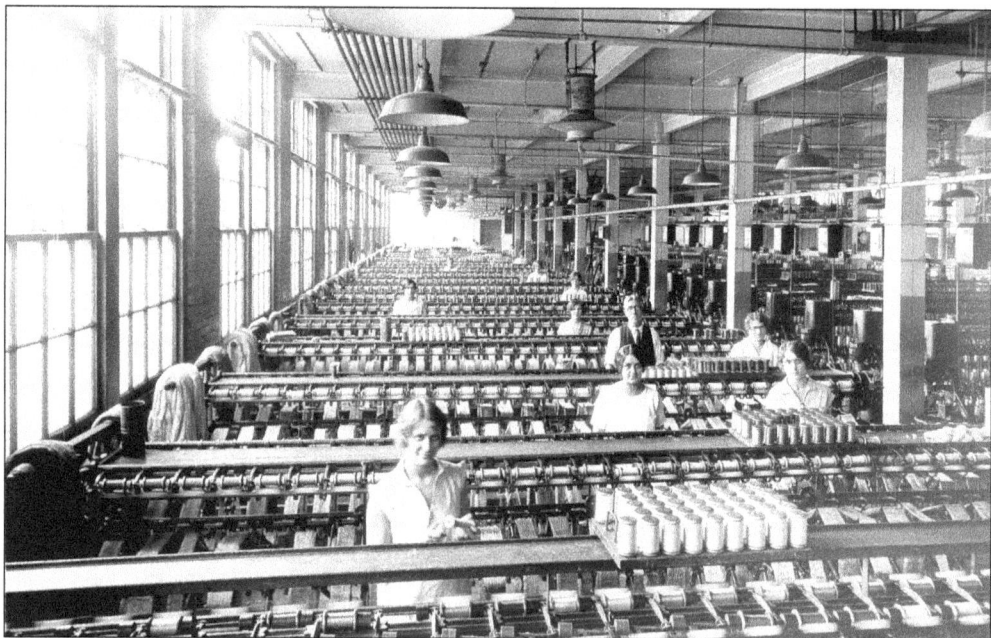

Winding frames with rows of swifts wound the silk into spools. Women workers oversaw the process at stations in front of the winding frames. The spools are located at the top of the machines.

Women workers paid close attention to the bobbins in the spinning rooms, shown in this c. 1926 photograph. One woman who worked in the Skinner Mills during the 1920s stated "we used to dress up to kill. The Skinners' girls were all very well-dressed girls. You couldn't go in there not dressed up nice . . . that was the Skinner motto. That girls had to be well dressed."

To create warp yarns on a loom for weaving fabric, silk yarns were measured by a warping creel. The creel's framework supported thousands of silk yarns and prevented them from becoming tangled. The weft yarns were woven through the warp yarns. These women worked in the quilling room in 1928.

This is the winding and spinning department at William Skinner and Sons Manufacturing Company around 1925. Women were largely employed in silk mills under the supervision of male overseers.

To weave cloth, warp yarns are parallel to each other and tied from the back to the front of the loom under tension. There are two harnesses, each threaded with every other warp yarn. Skinner satin was woven in a four to one ratio, with each warp yarn floated over four wefts, under one. The company weavers threaded five harnesses, each threaded with every fifth yarn of warp. When the weaver raises one harness, one half of the warp yarns lift. When the weaver raises the other harness, the other half of the warp yarn is lifted.

To create the Skinner name in the selvage, a dobby attachment was woven into the yarn. The dobby operated additional harnesses by means of wooden slats or by a perforated card. This woman is working the warping machine.

Emma Zahn (left) and her co-worker Atta Pittroff Lemke (front right) weave silk on two looms. Their foreman was Bob Stopgeshoff.

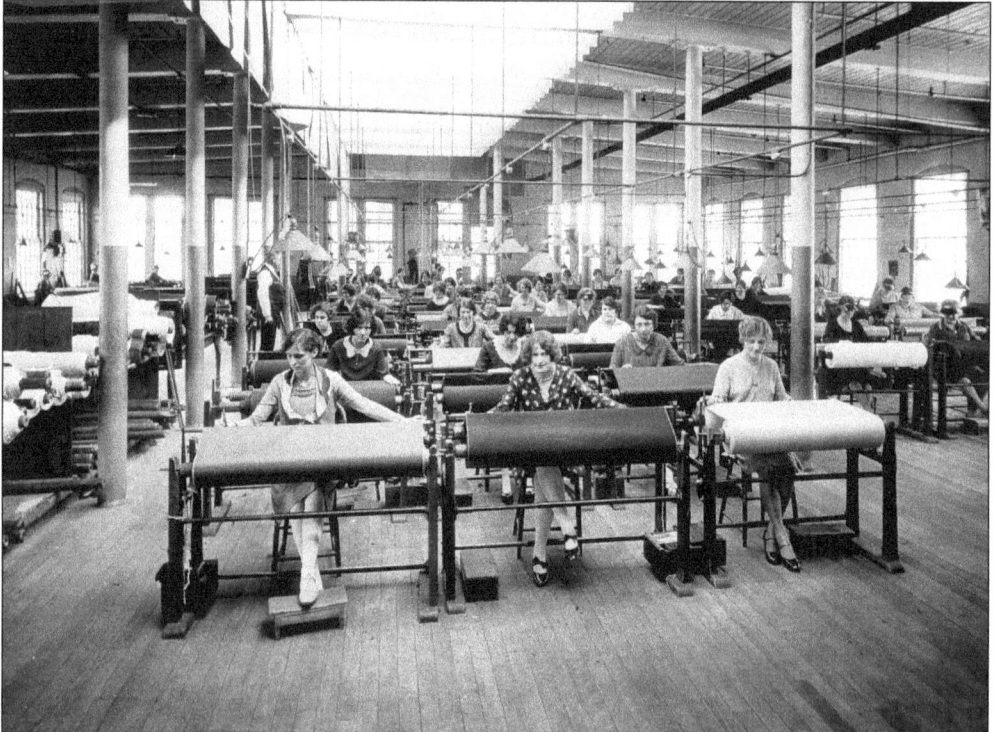

After the weaver was done, the cloth was inspected. Inspectors examined the silk cloth after it was produced. William Skinner and Sons Manufacturing Company was renowned for high-quality silk.

In the 1920s, William Skinner had a plant on Bond Street, where this woman worked in the inspecting room. Skinner's markets focused on wedding silks and satins, which included ring pillows, veils, gowns, and shoes. Skinner products ranged from silk, suede, and satin to crepe fabrics and included jackets, jacket linings, shoes, blanket covers, and undergarments.

Christine Keller worked on inspecting the finished cloth. Her foreman was Frank Folta, inspecting bundled cloth in the back left.

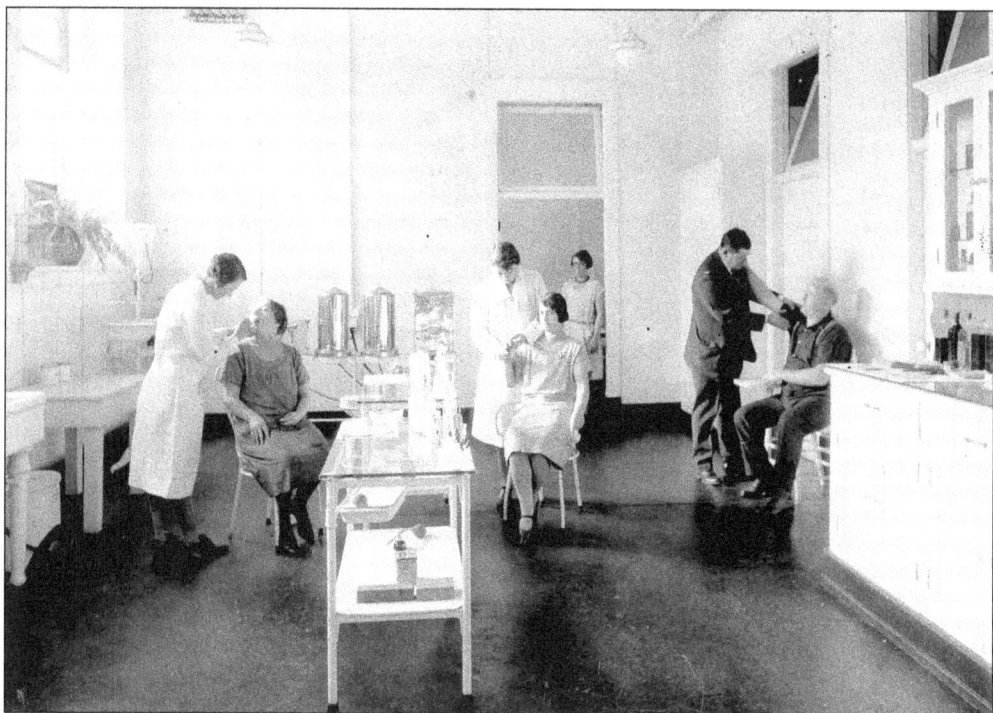
Dr. Cox was the doctor at the Skinner Silk Mill Infirmary.

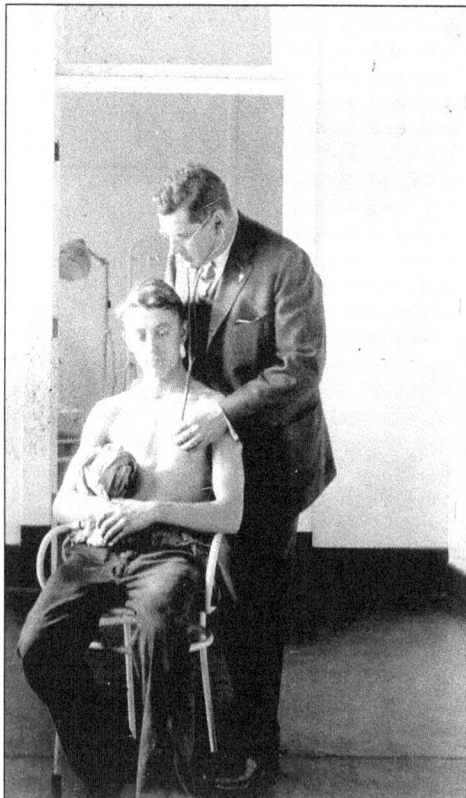

Along with providing basic care at the infirmary, it has been said that during the Depression, the Skinners would tell the hospital to bill them directly if one of their workers was taken to the hospital.

Joseph Skinner, shown here in his Holyoke Office in the 1930s, began work as the treasurer of William Skinner and Sons Manufacturing Company, and he worked closely with his brother William C., often traveling to Europe and Japan to learn new manufacturing techniques.

The Skinners purchased raw silk from Gunze. On April 21, 1913, two days after the main plant of the Gunze Silk Manufacturing Company caught fire, Joseph Skinner visited Ayabe, Japan.

By 1902, annual revenues for the company were $6.5 million. In 1937, the mills were recovering from the Depression, as were most factories nationwide. When William C. Skinner died in 1946, the mills were closed for 24 hours in respect of him. He was remembered as a daring and ambitious financier, as well as a friendly and genial gentleman who always carried a cane and wore a red silk tie and blue suit.

The company remained largely in family hands, as indicated by this photograph, which shows Robert Stewart Kilborne, Roland Brindamour, Frank Folta, William Hubbard, and Richard Beuchel inspecting draper machines at the Dwight Street plant in 1938. In 1934, Skinner launched a synthetic fabric department, which made underwear, linings, and dress fabrics. Many specialized and innovative fabrics were developed over the years and carried the Skinner name for quality and reputation.

The man with five daughters

has a keen realization of the cost of living. He doesn't always say so, but in his heart he wants good value with every family purchase.

Whether you are an only daughter or one of five, you can help father out by using Skinner's Silks.

Skinner's gives so much more than is ordinarily considered good silk service that every yard you buy means economy.

Skinner wearing quality is a live, pertinent fact, not merely a 72-year-old tradition.

"Look for the Name in the Selvage"

Ask for Skinner's "404" All-Silk for gowns, blouses, petticoats skirts or undergarments.

WILLIAM SKINNER & SONS

Established 1848

New York   Boston   Philadelphia   Chicago
Mills, Holyoke, Mass.

Skinner's
SILKS and SATINS
(36 inches wide)

"LOOK FOR THE NAME IN THE SELVAGE"

Over the 87 years of operation in Holyoke, William Skinner and Sons Manufacturing Company made an array of fabrics from its earliest products of silk, cotton-backed satin, and pure-dye taffetas to washable crepes, rayon, and tackle twill. Most popular among the later lines of Skinner materials was bridal satin, remembered today by many brides of the 1940s and 1950s. In 1961, the Skinner family sold the business, with all their trademarks and patents, to Indian Head Mills, which closed the mills a year later. At the time of the sale, Skinner and Sons was Holyoke's oldest family-owned and operated business. By the end of the 1960s, however, the plant closed and the building was sold.

The mill buildings were destroyed by a fire in 1980. Investigators believed youngsters playing in the empty mill building set the fire. The old mill site is currently Holyoke Heritage State Park. (Copyright 2005 The Republican Company. All rights reserved. Reprinted with permission.)

Five

BELLE SKINNER'S WISTARIAHURST

When William and Sarah Skinner died, Belle Skinner and her eldest brother William C. Skinner, both unmarried, inherited the house. Soon after, Belle began an extensive remodeling of the interior and exterior. Today, the house reflects the tastes of two generations of the Skinner family. Electricity was installed in 1905. The house always had indoor plumbing and central heat.

No room was more important than the parlor for entertaining guests. The parlor was a space used for displaying artwork, furniture, and rugs. The parlor created a setting in which guests were surrounded by objects that reflected the wealth and cultured taste of their host. When William and Sarah Skinner lived there, the room was dark with heavy drapes and elaborate wallpaper.

By the time Belle Skinner inherited the house, the cluttered parlor of her parents' era was highly undesirable. She hired contractors to make the room over in a more fashionable style, placing columns where the dividing wall once stood and adding lighter-colored wallpaper. She added a decorative wall border. She bought her first instrument, a Rutgers harpsichord, in 1906 or 1907, and housed it in the parlor before building the music room.

The leather room was originally William Skinner's bedroom. After his death in 1902, his children used it as a study. Belle had the walls covered in Spanish leather, with ornament of floral design. The work cost a total of over $2,000 in 1914.

When she added the breakfast room and music room, Belle Skinner designed the dining room to have bow windows and oak paneling, with the wallpaper above the paneling made of silk. She loved to entertain. She kept a book of seating arrangements in order to balance the guests.

William and Sarah Skinner added a study to the second floor of the house in 1898. When Belle Skinner inherited the house, she converted this space to a second place for her musical instruments, the first being the parlor. When her musical instruments were relocated to the music room, she used this space as a small study and sitting room. It was perhaps the site of the first radio at Wistariahurst. In many ways, this room represents the increasing technological changes of the 20th century. The telephone, radio, and wireless cable had a profound affect on Americans because it brought the world into their homes. For people who traveled extensively, like the Skinners, these changes helped keep news flowing and assured the safety of family members.

The music room was constructed in 1914 specifically to house Belle Skinner's large and growing collection of unique musical instruments. She had 89 rare instruments from the 1500s, 1600s, and 1700s, including harps, harpsichords, spinets, and stringed instruments, along with a Stradivarius violin and drums. Collecting was a popular hobby among the wealthy, and Belle used her travels throughout the world as an excuse to seek out rare instruments. The collection is now housed in Yale University's Collection of Musical Instruments in New Haven, Connecticut.

This unidentified woman in the 1950s was playing one of the harpsichords in Belle Skinner's instrument collection. While Katharine Skinner lived at Wistariahurst in the 1950s, the music collection was open for visiting. Fanny Reed Hammond gave tours of the room and had extensive knowledge of the instrument collection.

With windows dominating both exterior walls, the conservatory was a natural spot for Belle Skinner's plants and birds. Before the house was given to the city of Holyoke, its flat roof had decorative railings and was used as a rooftop porch, accessible from a second-floor room. The peacock window is one of two that graced this room and is said to be from the Tiffany studio in New York. The room was called the breakfast room when Katharine Skinner lived here with her family.

In 1927, Belle Skinner hired an architect from Philadelphia to design a new entranceway for Wistariahurst. The new entrance reoriented the front from Pine Street to Cabot Street and added an elegant porte cochere. Belle purchased shale fossil stones laden with dinosaur tracks to pave the driveway. The dinosaur tracks had been recently discovered in Holyoke, and were purchased from Murray's Stone Quarry.

In 1927, after Belle Skinner completed the great hall addition to the house, she held a family reunion with her siblings and their children. They set a large table in front of the fireplace and made a toast to the Skinner name and family loyalty while they passed around their parents' 40th-anniversary cup filled with wine.

Belle Skinner's renovations included the great hall and a marble lobby. She and her brother William enjoyed entertaining, and this grand space was central to the entertainment of friends and family. Her plans in the great hall included the construction of a French Beaux Arts staircase. The design on the iron railing is of peonies that slowly open as the stairs ascend.

The French doors that open onto the back porch from the library were originally the main entrance to Wistariahurst. Because Belle Skinner's social peers were building up the hill in Holyoke, Pine Street was no longer considered a fashionable address, so she moved the entrance. The room was originally two separate rooms, the original hall and a library. It included a dividing wall that once stood where the columns are.

The porch facing Pine Street was reconstructed in 1927 by Casper Ranger Construction Company of Holyoke. Katharine Skinner always referred to the porch as the piazza.

The Oriental bedroom is decorated with objects from the Orient and was used as a guest bedroom by Katharine's son Stewart and his wife, Barbara. In 1925, Stewart was attending Yale and wanted to announce his engagement to Barbara Briggs. But Yale's policy forbade undergraduate students to be married. Katharine and her husband agreed, stating they wanted Stewart to finish his studies. Rather than wait, however, he and Barbara eloped. When Belle added this room to the house, she had them in mind.

This room was originally Sarah Skinner's room. When she died in 1908, it became Belle Skinner's most private space, symbolizing her authority as woman of the house. She hired Casper Ranger Construction Company of Holyoke to install a new hardwood floor and update the room. She had a taste for antiques and combined furniture from many different time periods in her room. The view from these windows overlooks her rose gardens.

Belle Skinner inherited her mother, Sarah's, love of gardening and followed her example by carefully tending to the details of the grounds. While her mother favored groves of trees and shrubs, Belle enjoyed the formally laid out perennial gardens. She also scattered statuary throughout the gardens.

Belle Skinner hired Wadley and Smyth of New York City in 1909 to design her perennial garden. In 1914, she hired Boston landscape architect Herbert Kellaway to design a rose garden. She took her gardens very seriously and studied many other gardens as well. In 1910, she wrote, "The most charming path I ever saw . . . the Wild Thyme—common herb—bordering a path in a kitchen garden . . . it is so delightfully informal and perfectly natural . . . but a group here and there on the flower border margin is most welcome. Most exquisite of all is the Gentianella (gentiana scaulis), . . . blooms of intense blue, that arise from a carpet of dwarft leafage." She used her observations to develop her individual tastes and applied them to the gardens at Wistariahurst.

Belle Skinner installed several fountains, a koi pond, and statuary.

As impressive as Wistariahurst was becoming, Belle Skinner and her eldest brother William used it more as a second home in the mid- to late 1920s, making their full-time residence in New York City. Katharine and her husband, Robert Kilborne, also had a home in New York City. This is a photograph looking from the Kilborne parlor to the library on the second floor; the stairs go up to the third floor, where their bedrooms were. The children had bedrooms on the fourth floor, and the maids' rooms were on the fifth floor.

Six

HOUSEHOLD STAFF

Maintaining Wistariahurst required the labor of many housekeepers, nurses, nannies, gardeners, butlers, chauffeurs, and other maintenance staff. These women and men worked daily to keep the household running smoothly. (Courtesy of Sarah Skinner Kilborne.)

The waitress in this photograph from around 1900 is wearing an evening uniform and attending to children at tea on the porch. Records show that over the years there were at least seven known butlers and seven known waitresses who worked at Wistariahurst. (Courtesy of Sarah Skinner Kilborne.)

An informal picnic around 1900 is held with waitresses in attendance. The picnic blanket is still dressed with floral arrangements, and the food is served on china dishes. The man kneeling in the background is Robert Stewart Kilborne. (Courtesy of Sarah Skinner Kilborne.)

This is a wall separating the servants' entrance and workspace from the public entrance to the house off of Beech Street. Here, the servants hung laundry and repaired vehicles. The wall kept the servants' area out of view from those coming up the driveway to the porte cochere and main entrance.

✝ HATTIE RILEY ✝
BORN · HARROWGATE · ENGLAND ·
· MARCH · 2 · 1848 ·
· DIED · HOLYOKE · MASSACHUSETTS ·
· DECEMBER · 14 · 1926 ·

· IN · REMEMBRANCE · OF ·
· 47 · YEARS · OF · FAITHFUL · SERVICE ·

The position of housekeeper was the highest-ranking position for women among household staff. The housekeeper managed all the female workers except the cook. Wistariahurst had several housekeepers, including two who worked for the family for over 50 years. Hattie Riley (1848–1926) worked first as a maid and then as the family's housekeeper in the early 1900s. She was the only servant to be buried with the family at Forestdale Cemetery.

Wealthy families commonly hired trained nurses to attend the ill and elderly in their homes. The trained nurse commanded respect and was given a high level of responsibility because she was a professional. The trained nurse provided round-the-clock care to the patient, administering medicines and therapies prescribed by the doctor. She might also cook meals for patients on restricted diets, change bed linens, and bathe the patients. The nurse would always wear the cap of her nursing school. Hulda Klemm (1869–1950) (center) graduated with the first nursing class to complete training at Holyoke Hospital in 1895. She was hired to care for Sarah Skinner but worked for the family for five decades. She is pictured with her classmates Ella Poole (left) and Florence Stickley.

Trained nurses sometimes insisted that they would only perform nursing duties and would not be responsible for household cleaning. To a nurse, agreeing to do the work of a maid lowered her status and damaged her reputation as a trained professional. Although Hulda Klemm was a trained nurse, by the 1930s, she was promoted to housekeeper.

In 1907, Sarah Skinner wrote to her daughter Katharine Skinner Kilborne, "She [Belle] is poorly enough yet but we have Klemm taking care of her and as we have confidence in her so think all will be well done." After Sarah's death in 1908, Hulda Klemm stayed on to provide care for Belle and, later, for Katharine Skinner Kilborne's children.

Charles Linderme, a chauffeur for the family, described Hulda Klemm (left, holding a squirrel) as "strict, but honest, fair. . . . She was always right." She was very close to the family and even kept a scrapbook of all Belle's accomplishments. In 1950, Katharine Skinner Kilborne wrote of her passing, "Miss Klemm, the housekeeper and my dear friend of mine and my children, was found dead, . . . She was faithful until death." (Courtesy of Sarah Skinner Kilborne.)

Unlike the trained nurse, the nanny or nursemaid was not usually a trained professional. More often, she had a long relationship with a particular family and was promoted to the job of nursemaid. The position of a nanny or nursemaid was a live-in job. These women were on call 24 hours a day and traveled with the family. (Courtesy of Sarah Skinner Kilborne.)

Ruth, Elizabeth, William, and nursemaid Grace Slater traveled to Manchester, England. It is believed that Grace Slater was a nursemaid for the Skinner family while the children were young. Servants were often engaged in family exploits. Katharine Skinner Kilborne writes in her journal of 1889, "Grace stayed all night with me and we dressed up a ghost on mamma's dress-form and frightened the servants nearly to death." (Courtesy of William Bicknell.)

Although she started as a chambermaid and then served as a nursemaid, Nellie Wright (right) eventually became a personal companion to Katharine Skinner Kilborne. On Saturday, July 22, 1944, Katharine wrote in her diary, "Nellie Wright is my greatest joy in the home . . . [she] is always pleasant and very efficient." This photograph was taken at one of Katharine's birthday parties. Also pictured is Betty Kilborne, Katharine's daughter-in-law. (Courtesy of Allerton Kilborne.)

The Skinner family occasionally hired tutors for their children. Here, Robert Stewart Kilborne Jr. and an unknown girl are studying in a room. (Courtesy of Sarah Skinner Kilborne.)

Chauffeurs traveled extensively with the family. George Brakey (1873–1931) (pictured) had a certain run-in with William C. Skinner. William C. wrote in his journal, "George took our beautiful black horse Stanley and went to dinner at his brother's in Easthampton yesterday and coming home . . . [Stanley fell] into a hole and broke one of his back legs so he had to be killed—I'm mad with George he is so awful shiftless." (Courtesy of Sarah Skinner Kilborne.)

Though George Brakey later became the chauffeur, he was also charged with the care of the pony, Relief, acquired by the Skinners in 1906. (Courtesy of William Bicknell.)

George Brakey's son Walter (right) took over the job of chauffeur. He remained on staff until he joined the army and went to war in 1942.

In 1945, housekeeper Hulda Klemm hired local musician Charles Linderme (1949–1990), shown here with Nellie Wright, as a full-time chauffeur. Linderme served as chauffeur to Katharine Skinner Kilborne and took charge of managing the house during the 1950s. He lived in a small apartment in the carriage house, and when he moved to his own apartment, Katharine paid his rent. Linderme called Katharine "the Chief," a title that no other staff member was allowed to use. Linderme adored Katharine and Wistariahurst. He died in 1990, and his funeral cortege circled Wistariahurst twice before he was laid to rest.

The cook was in command of the kitchen, controlling all food preparation, from ordering produce, meat, fish, and groceries to cooking all meals and supervising the kitchen maid. In a household like Wistariahurst, the cook was expected to make three meals a day and supply enough food for the family and staff. Pictured here are Emma Peeples (left), Ada Peoples, and Charles Linderme. Katharine Skinner Kilborne marked in her diary, "a faithful cook" Ada Peoples died on March 12, 1961. (Courtesy of Allerton Kilborne.)

Wistariahurst's three acres of grounds required the constant attention of a crew of gardeners supervised by a head gardener. Edward Haczynski (pictured) was a gardener for Katharine Skinner Kilborne in 1959. She gave him her favorite wicker rocking chair when she left Holyoke. (Courtesy of Allerton Kilborne.)

Personal companion, or maid-companion, was a special position at Wistariahurst. The personal companion served the woman of the household and was not responsible to any other member of the family or staff. She did not dress in a uniform and accompanied her mistress on all her travels. Both Belle Skinner and Katharine Skinner Kilborne employed personal companions who stayed with them for many years.

Prudence Lagogue (1880?–1967) was hired by Belle Skinner in 1910 to travel to Europe as a companion. She lived with Belle in France, New York, and Holyoke. She provided assistance with Belle's endeavor to reconstruct the French village of Hattonchatel. She also attended to Belle's correspondence and managed her social calendar. (Courtesy of Allerton Kilborne.)

Prudence Lagogue (pictured) and Belle Skinner owned at least one Great Dane in Hattonchatel, France. (Courtesy of William Bicknell.)

Both Prudence Lagogue and William C. Skinner attended the 1928 dedication of the memorial plaque to Belle Skinner in Hattonchatel. Here, they are standing in front of the chateau of Hattonchatel. (Courtesy of William Bicknell.)

In Belle Skinner's will, she decreed that Prudence Lagogue get $15,000; Jean Wright, another housekeeper, $2,500; George Brakey, $2,500; and Hattie Riley and Mary Bresnahan, $1,000. Supporting staff like nurses, housekeepers, and chauffeurs were not merely staff but also a part of the family.

Seven

THE SKINNER FAMILY IN THE COMMUNITY

William Skinner was actively engaged in Holyoke's charitable and philanthropic needs. In 1891, he and William Whiting worked to establish a hospital in Holyoke, which was dedicated in 1893. Both gave $5,000 to start a fund for the Holyoke Hospital. Skinner was a trustee of the Holyoke Public Library and donated $10,000 toward the Holyoke Public Library Fund. He also helped educational institutions like Mount Holyoke, Smith, and Vassar Colleges and also built a gymnasium for the Northfield Seminary in Northfield. (Courtesy of William Bicknell.)

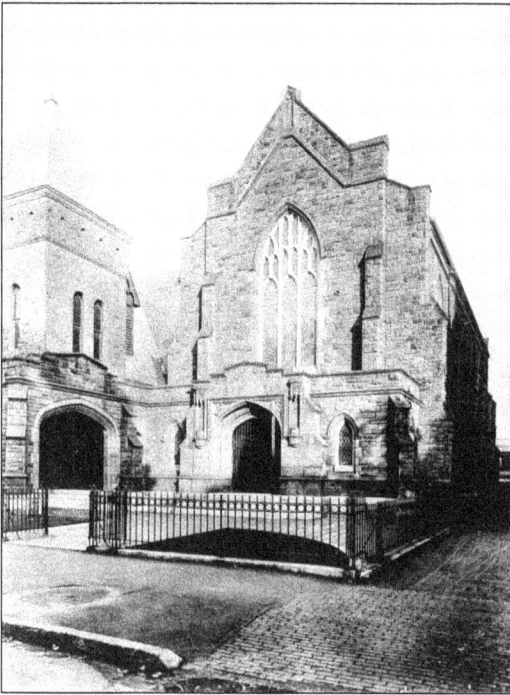

In memory of their parents, the children of William and Sarah Skinner gave and endowed the Skinner Memorial Chapel of the Second Congregational Church in Holyoke in 1909. The chapel, joined to the church and parish building, bears the dedication "To the Glory of God and in loving memory of William and Sarah E. Skinner."

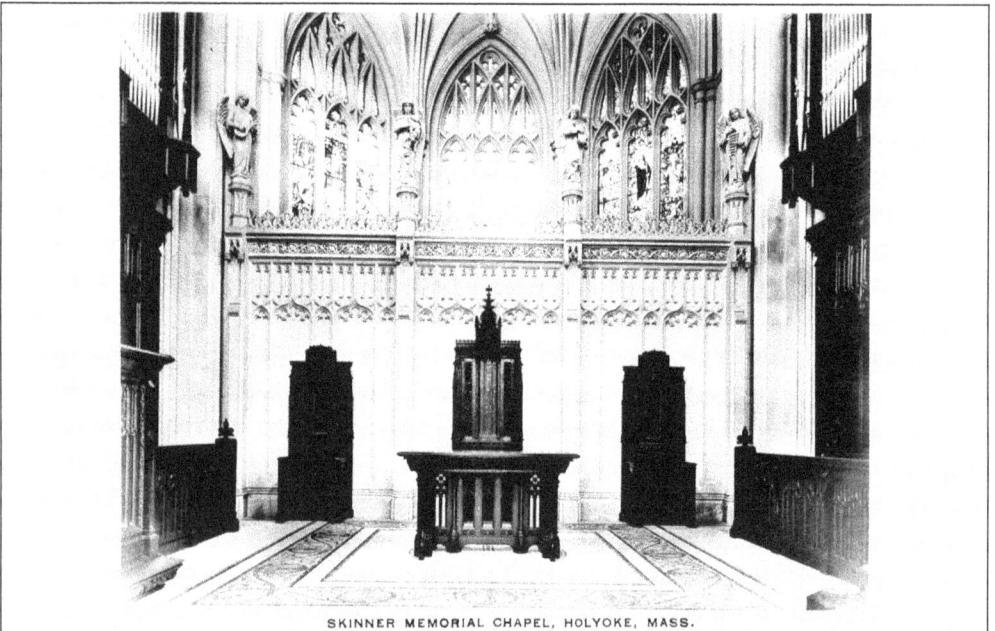

SKINNER MEMORIAL CHAPEL, HOLYOKE, MASS.

The chapel is one of the loveliest found among Congregational churches, and special services are sometimes held there.

The Skinner Coffee House stood at 480 Main Street, opposite the Holyoke Machine Shop in a store formerly occupied by Lemuel Sears and Company. It was established in 1902 by Belle and Katharine Skinner in honor of their father, William Skinner. The coffeehouse was one of many settlement houses established throughout the country around 1900 to serve the needs of recent immigrants, especially women, who worked in mills and factories.

In 1916, the Skinner Coffee House moved to 402 Main Street and continued to serve the community under the Skinner family until 1942. The city continued to run the Skinner Community House at the same location until 1989. This photograph of the Mother's Club, which met at the coffeehouse, was taken on June 18, 1919.

The Women's Club met at the Skinner Coffee House, as shown here in 1949. Seen in this photograph are the following, Mary Greco, Gina Tonelli, Mary Martinelli, Bruna Conti, Terisina Bertani, Zaria Grumoli, Rose Mazzolini, Mrs. Clark, Inez Cerruti, Josie Batastini, Amedea Cavani, Mrs. Del Totto, Mrs. Potrois, Dorothy Franz, and Mrs. Griffin.

The Women's Club enjoyed lunch in 1948, when the building was the Skinner Community Center. Besides providing a place for clubs to meet, it was a refuge in times of emergency. During a flood in the 1930s, the coffeehouse provided Gloria Fortin's family a place to stay. Susan Van Riper, the director at that time, took care of the family. According to a little girl who attended the coffeehouse, "We called her Grandma because she took us under her wing."

The Skinner Coffee House provided coffee and sandwiches for a small price in its cafeteria. For example, soup was 7¢ and mashed potatoes, corn, spinach, apricot pie, and cookies were 5¢ each. Women from the mills would spend their lunch hour and time after work there.

This photograph shows the Here Comes the Bride pageant in 1937. More than 20 clubs and organizations utilized the Skinner Coffee House. Along with pageants and musical revues, organizations created a community through regularly scheduled meetings and luncheons. Many girls joined the same clubs years after their mothers were involved. Education was also an integral part of the coffeehouse's mission and included programs for both adults and children. These programs fulfilled practical and recreational needs. Some of the educational opportunities were dancing, English instruction, singing, knitting, physical education, quilting, piano lessons, and reading.

Jennifer Roberts, at age 17, stands still as her sister-in-law, Joyce, hems a senior prom dress. This was taken at the Skinner Community House before a fashion show in 1987. Proceeds benefited the after-school playground for girls ages six and up.

Jeanne Plouffe (at the mantel) and Jennie Finn (left) tidied the area for the bazaar, which also served as the house's 80th anniversary. The Skinner Community Center, headed by director Anita Healey, held a bazaar in November 1982. The service organizations at the Skinner Coffee House also undertook projects on national and international levels. Locally, women raised money for charities like the American Red Cross.

These women of the Women's Club of the Skinner Coffee House and Community Center celebrate its 60th anniversary. Belle Skinner wrote and delivered a speech at the coffeehouse, thanking the women for their efforts in making garments for Hattonchatel. "It is always a pleasure for me to be with you. Even if I can't call myself a Coffee House girl, I am at least a Coffee House old lady, and I like to feel that I have a part in your life here."

Sally Johnson, program assistant Margaret Fallon, Iris Cruz, Judy Lopen, and Katie Healy are shown waiting for a bus to take them to the Springfield Museums and Planetarium in 1975. Afterward, they enjoyed a meal and ice cream at Friendly's Ice-Cream Shop. In the 1970s, the Skinner Community House was open after school to girls ages 6 to 16.

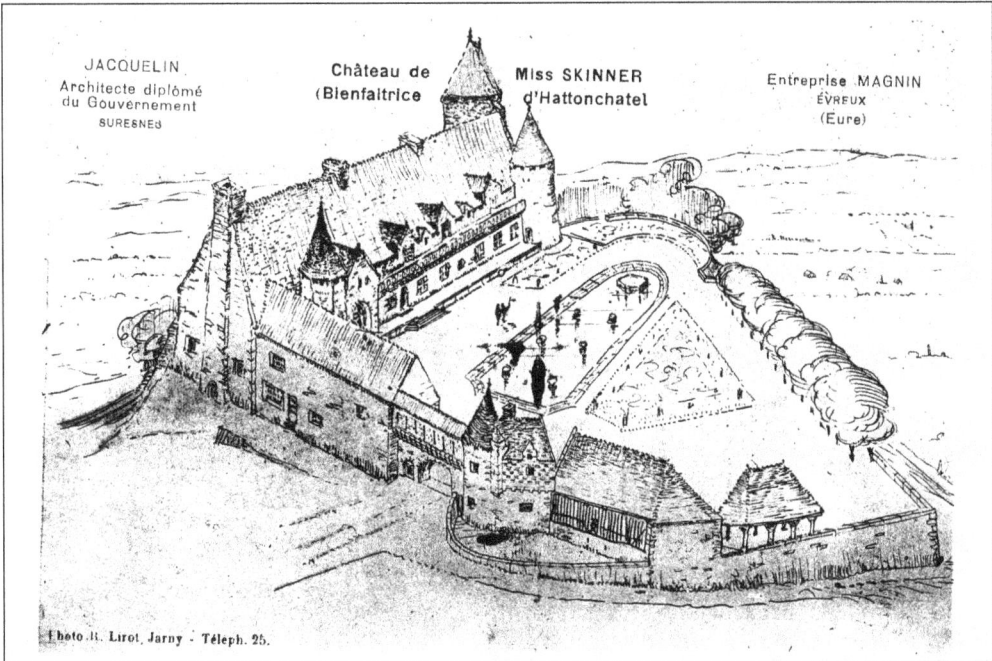

JACQUELIN
Architecte diplômé
du Gouvernement
SURESNES

Château de
(Bienfaitrice

Miss SKINNER
d'Hattonchatel

Entreprise MAGNIN
ÉVREUX
(Eure)

Photo R. Lirot, Jarny · Téléph. 25.

Belle Skinner focused her benevolent energies in France. After the Germans invaded France in 1918, taking the village of Hattonchatel without resistance and occupying it for four years, she organized the American Committee of the Villages Liberes and was its president during World War I. Following the war, she funded the reconstruction of the French village of Hattonchatel.

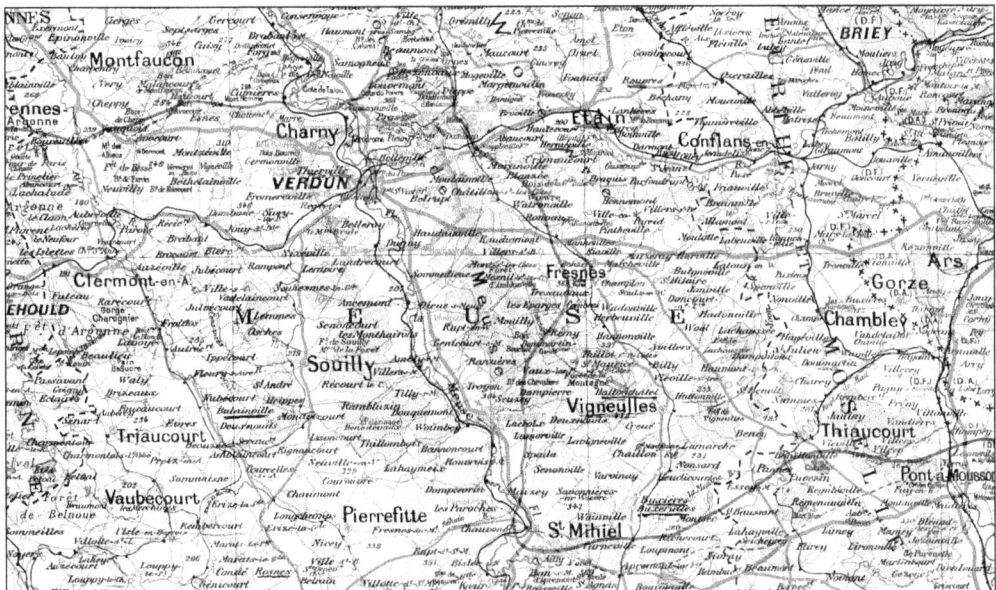

The population of Hattonchatel before German troops invaded was 162. While only 12 men of Hattonchatel were killed in the invasion, the village was virtually destroyed. The U.S. troops in the Saint-Michiel offensive drove the Germans out of Hattonchatel.

Before rebuilding, the debris from the war had to be cleared away. The shell holes and trenches had to be filled in, and the barbed wire had to be cut and rolled up. Villagers lived in temporary shelters while Belle Skinner secured a supply of chickens, ducks, horses, cattle, seed, and tools.

Belle Skinner (right) made sure that the village had a water supply, money to repair the town hall, and a schoolhouse, as well as electricity. (Courtesy of William Bicknell.)

At least six markers in Hattonchatel recognize Belle Skinner's work. In recognition of her endeavors, the French government bestowed upon her the Gold Medal of the Reconnaissance Francaise in 1919 and the Cross of the Legion d'Honneur in 1920.

Welcoming visitors into the village is a monument to mothers who lost their sons in war.

Belle Skinner is buried in the family plot at Forestdale Cemetery, just up the hill from Wistariahurst. Upon her death, the village of Hattonchatel wrote a poem for her entitled "Her Bells."

Across the seas
We can hear them ringing--
Bells of Apremont,
Of Hatton-Chattel and St. Maur--
Ringing for Easter,
And for her,
Their friend:
For to their early ringing
Over the sweet fields of France,
Out of the dawn rose and gray,
In and out of sky-larks' singing,
Her loyal, gallant soul
Went winging
On its way.

To that far ringing
In her loved France,
Here at home
Our hearts are listening,
As if every bell
In every busy mill
And every spire of prayer
Here in the city that loves her,
Had caught the resonance;
And all the April air
Thrills and chimes
With thought of her,
Resounds
Through sunlit showers,
Remembering.

Belle Skinner was familiar with village and military politics. Here, she stands with General Berthelot while overseeing the restoration of Hattonchatel. In 1928, when traveling to the village, she contracted pneumonia and died.

William C. Skinner, Belle Skinner, and Katharine and Robert Kilborne attended a dinner hosted by the France-American Society in honor of His Excellency Ferdinand Foch, marshal of France, at the Waldorf Astoria in New York in 1921.

Joseph Skinner built the Orchards Golf Course in South Hadley for his daughter Elisabeth. He contracted Donald Ross to design a nine-hole golf course in 1922, and the second nine holes were added in 1927. In the summer of 1941, he commented of his golf course that "the lawn has been mowed as also the putting green flower beds trimmed and everything looks beautifully. It seems as though I have never seen the place so fine."

Elisabeth Skinner took up golf and became one of the top golfers in New England, winning the Endicott Cup twice. She is pictured here in 1919.

Elisabeth Skinner held the Orchards course record (74) for 40 years. She enclosed this photograph in a letter to her mother, Martha Skinner, in August 1905. She and her father would often practice by hitting a few golf balls in the backyard of their home in South Hadley. Established in 1933, her course record was from the men's tees because there were no women's tees at the time. Pat Bradley (Ladies Professional Golf Association) broke that record in 1973 with a score of 73.

William Skinner II and his father, Joseph, practiced their golf swings.

Upon his death, Joseph Skinner bequeathed his South Hadley home to Mount Holyoke College, with the stipulation that his daughter Elisabeth could live there until her death. In her later years, she was insistent that she live on her own but hired a driver who ran errands. She died in September 1987 at the age of 95. The estate is now the home of the Berkshire Hills Academy of Music.

Wistariahurst, now an historic house museum, features original leather wall coverings, elaborate woodwork, and an interesting tale of how two generations perceived and used the house very differently. The museum's permanent collection includes decorative arts, paintings and prints, textiles, and a rich manuscript collection of family and local papers. Wistariahurst Museum offers a wide variety of programs and events including workshops, concerts, lectures, and demonstrations.

128

Visit us at
arcadiapublishing.com

www.ingramcontent.com/pod-product-compliance
Lightning Source LLC
Chambersburg PA
CBHW050635110426
42813CB00007B/1813

* 9 7 8 1 5 3 1 6 2 3 5 1 7 *